W9-AET-856

The Many Kinds of Cold

by Dale-Marie Bryan

Ideas for Parents and Teachers

Amicus Readers let children practice reading informational texts at the earliest reading levels. Familiar words and concepts with close photo-text matches support early readers.

Before Reading

- Discuss the cover photo with the child. What does it tell him?
- Ask the child to predict what she will learn in the book.

Read the Book

- "Walk" through the book and look at the photos. Let the child ask questions.
- Read the book to the child, or have the child read independently.

After Reading

- Use the picture glossary at the end of the book to review the text.
- Prompt the child to make connections. Ask: What are other words for cold?

Amicus Readers are published by Amicus
P.O. Box 1329, Mankato, MN 56002
www.amicuspublishing.us

Library of Congress
Cataloging-in-Publication Data
Bryan, Dale-Marie, 1953-
 The many kinds of cold / Dale-Marie Bryan.
  pages cm. -- (So Many Synonyms)
 ISBN 978-1-60753-511-9 (hardcover) -- ISBN 978-1-60753-538-6 (eBook)
 1. English language--Synonyms and antonyms--Juvenile literature. I. Title.
 PE1591.B763 2013
 428.1--dc23
                    2013010404

Photo Credits: Shutterstock Images, cover, 1, 14, 15, 16 (bottom right); Dirk Ercken/Shutterstock Images, 3; Markus Mainka/Shutterstock Images, 4, 16 (top left); Mosley Images/Shutterstock Images, 6, 7, 16 (middle left); Elen Studio/Shutterstock Images, 9, 16 (bottom left); M. Unal Ozmen/Shutterstock Images, 11, 16 (top right); Laura Stone/Shutterstock Images, 12, 16 (middle right)

Produced for Amicus by The Peterson Publishing Company and Red Line Editorial.

Editor Jenna Gleisner
Designer Becky Daum
Printed in the United States of America
Mankato, MN
1-2014
PO1192
10 9 8 7 6 5 4 3 2

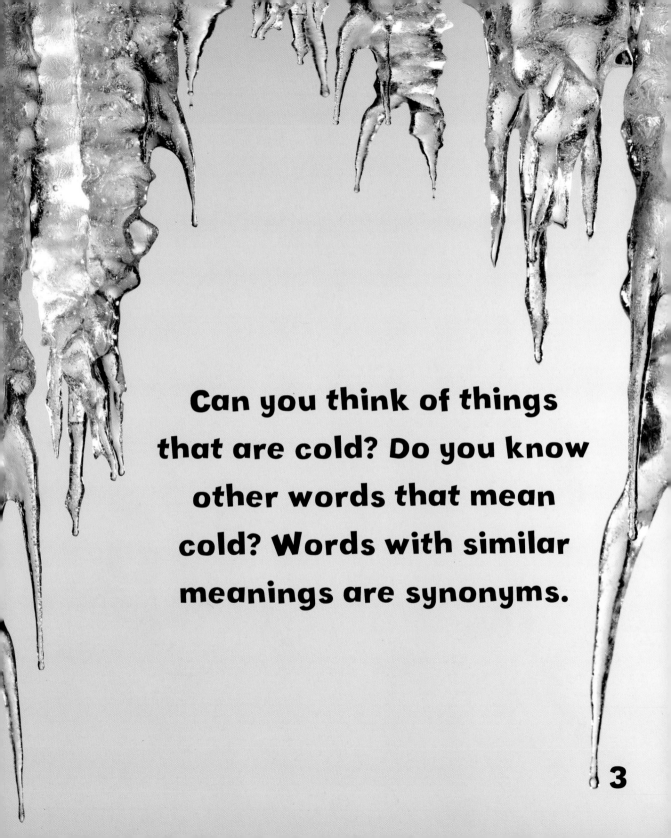

Can you think of things that are cold? Do you know other words that mean cold? Words with similar meanings are synonyms.

3

4

Cool means cold.

Ice cubes keep lemonade cool on a summer day. We will serve lemonade by the pool.

Crisp means cold.

The air feels crisp when the temperature falls. Warm breath looks like fog in the crisp air.

Chilly means cold.

We pack chilly snow together to make a snowman. Later, we will put a red scarf on the snowman.

Frosty means cold.

Ice cream stays frosty in the freezer. The most common flavor is vanilla.

11

Freezing means cold.

Water turns to solid ice when it is freezing cold. The ice at the skating rink is shaped like an oval.

Frigid means cold.

The South Pole is frigid.
It is the coldest place on Earth.
Is it cold where you live?

15

Synonyms for Cold

cool
a little cold

frosty
cold enough to make frost

crisp
cold and dry

freezing
cold enough to freeze water

chilly
cold

frigid
extremely cold